TAMPA

AND WEST CENTRAL FLORIDA

TAMPA

AND WEST CENTRAL FLORIDA

Postcard Paradise

THE TAMPA TRIBUNE

WITH THE UNIVERSITY OF TAMPA PRESS

— INTRODUCTION BY KATHY FEENEY

Welcome to a land of sand, soul and serendipity. Here, you can stroll along sugar-fine beaches and swim in sapphire surf, browse for best sellers in Florida's largest independent bookstore, and meet a gentle gray giant called a manatee. Picture yourself in a canoe on a river and don't forget to greet the alligator sunbathing on the bank nearby. Whether golf is your game or shopping seems more sporting, whether you crave Broadway shows or big band swing, whether you're mad for museums or nuts about nature, the Tampa Bay area is the perfect location for entertainment, education and escape. Along the way, you will see a diverse array of splendid scenery: strawberry fields, orange groves, rolling hills, verdant pastures, brilliant flowers, regal palms, rocky river beds, powdery sand beaches, sparkling waterways, Spanish moss cloaking towering oaks and flourishing city skylines. Home to more than 2 million Floridians — including jazz great Nat Adderly, wrestler "Hollywood" Hogan, NFL Hall-of-Famer Lee Roy Selmon and New York Yankees owner George Steinbrenner — the Tampa Bay area is a postcard paradise punctuated by spectacular sunsets.

Tampa has a temperate, semitropical climate with an average winter temperature of 62.5 degrees and an average summer

temperature of 81.4 degrees. On Florida's west coast, the region annually attracts millions of visitors from around the world who flock here to enjoy the beaches of St. Petersburg and Clearwater, and to experience Busch Gardens, Adventure Island, Ybor City, The Florida Aquarium, Lowry Park Zoo, MOSI (the Museum of Science & Industry) and major league sports including baseball, football, hockey and soccer.

Tampa's central location provides easy access to the beaches and some famous neighbors. Orlando is just 84 miles east of the Tampa Bay area. And small town serenity is a short drive away. In bucolic Brooksville, cows and horses graze in meadows as humans lunch in gourmet cafés and browse for antiques in nearby Dade City. Tarpon Springs, known as "The Sponge Capital of America," is like a day trip to Greece with its sponge docks, souvenir shops and waterside restaurants

serving specialties such as moussaka and baklava. Each January, Tarpon Springs boys jump into Spring Bayou to dive for the cross in observance of Epiphany. The youth who finds the cross is promised a year of good luck. Plant City, called "The Winter Strawberry Capital of the World," stages a strawberry festival every February, blending Southern hospitality with an array of strawberry concoctions and stellar entertainment that has included Kenny Rogers, Wayne Newton and Barbara Mandrell.

In 1997, 12.8 million passengers arrived and departed from Tampa International Airport (TIA), which ranks No. 1 among America's 36 largest airports, according to the Airline Passengers Association. Also, AAA named Tampa among the top five winter destinations in the United States. Compared with other Florida destinations, visitors described Tampa as "a good vacation value, not real touristy, relaxed, youthful, entertaining, accommodating and contemporary," in a survey conducted by the Tampa/Hillsborough Convention and Visitors Association Inc.

In Tampa you can start your day jogging on Bayshore Boulevard — often called the world's longest continuous sidewalk — and spend the afternoon swimming, fishing or boating in freshwater or saltwater lakes, rivers and bays. Evenings offer area bands performing reggae, rock, country, blues, jazz and swing.

Restaurants range from the laid-back island ambiance of Skipper's Smokehouse, where diners munch conch and gator, to Bern's Steak House, where the wine and dessert menus are as thick as telephone books and the European decor prompted America Eats Out magazine to call Bern's "the most remarkable restaurant in the entire world ... with gilded plaster columns, red wallpaper, Tiffany lamps and murals of French vineyards." Armani's, a northern Italian restaurant atop the Hyatt Regency Westshore, overlooks Old Tampa Bay and TIA with views of sunsets and takeoffs. Spanning a block on Seventh Avenue in Ybor City, the Columbia (built in 1905) is the oldest and largest Spanish restaurant in the U.S. Featuring a menu of classic Spanish and continental cuisine, the Columbia has served celebrities ranging from President Ronald Reagan to rock star Mick Jagger to actor John Wayne. Eating is an adventure in the Tampa Bay area. You can sample regional specialties such as stone crab claws, grouper and Key lime pie, or choose from an assortment of ethnic dishes including Indian, Vietnamese, Japanese, Chinese, Jamaican, Thai, Cuban, Cajun and Spanish cuisine.

The history of Tampa influences the flavor of the area. Originally an Indian fishing village, Tampa was a town with a population of 700 when Henry Bradley Plant extended his South Florida Railroad in 1884 and started a steamship line from here to Key

West to Havana. When Plant built his $3 million Moorish-style Tampa Bay Hotel in 1891 on the bank of the Hillsborough River, the Connecticut Yankee created an architectural treasure crowned by silver minarets that have become a much loved and photographed Tampa landmark. The city purchased the Tampa Bay Hotel in 1905 and it has served as the center of the University of Tampa since 1933. Now called Plant Hall, the building became a National Historic Landmark in 1977. A wing of the former hotel houses the Henry B. Plant Museum, furnished as it appeared in the late 1800s, and showcasing exhibits such as collections of French and Venetian mirrors and Oriental porcelain.

David P. Davis, another entrepreneur, helped shape the face of Tampa during the Florida land boom. In 1924, the real estate developer carved two mosquito-infested islands into a residential and commercial neighborhood. Today, Davis Islands boasts an airport, Tampa General Hospital and more than 100 of the original residential, recreational and commercial structures. Other people who have touched Tampa include Tony Jannus, who piloted the world's first regularly scheduled commercial airline flights from St. Petersburg to Tampa on Jan. 1, 1914, and baseball legend Babe Ruth, who hit his longest home run at Plant Field on April 4, 1919. Blues singer and pianist Ray Charles began his career performing in Tampa dance halls. In 1990, Charles received an honorary degree in music from the University of South Florida (USF). Actor Lauren Hutton grew up in Tampa and attended Chamberlain High School and USF before making it big in modeling. Ybor City native Al Lopez, whose nickname "El Señor" followed him through his career with the Pittsburgh Pirates, Brooklyn Dodgers, Boston Braves, Chicago White Sox and Cleveland Indians, was elected in 1977 to the Baseball Hall of Fame.

Tampa is nicknamed "The Big Guava" for the yellow, pear-shaped tropical fruit found in the city. Guavas are used for guava jelly, guava paste and pickled guavas.

Regenerated by an international resurgence in the popularity of cigars, Tampa is returning to its roots as the "Cigar City." During its heyday as the "Handmade Cigar Capital of the World," Ybor City employed nearly 12,000 workers in 200 factories. The area was settled by Cuban, Spanish, Italian, German and Jewish immigrants. Ybor City's cigar industry was founded by a Cuban exile named Vicente Martinez Ybor. Designated as one of only three National Historic districts in Florida, the Latin quarter showcases classic architecture, art galleries, boutiques, nightclubs and restaurants. Guided tours take travelers down red brick streets past wrought-iron balconies and globe street lamps to an era when immigrants rolled cigars by hand, and politicos and factory workers sat side-by-side in corner cafés dipping chunks of Cuban bread into steaming cups of café con leche. Each October, Ybor City hosts the Guavaween Parade and Festival, which attracts 100,000 revelers to Tampa's version of Halloween. Other celebrations include Ybor City's Fiesta Day, named one of the top 20 events in the South by the Southeast Tourism Society, and Tampa's Krewe of Sant' Yago Illuminated Night Parade, voted the largest and most beautiful night parade in the South and one of the top 10 parades in the Southeast by Suncoast Magazine.

Tampa is the only city in the world to be invaded every February by sinister, scar-faced pirates during the Gasparilla Parade and Pirate Fest, led by a legendary pirate named José Gaspar. In 1997, Events Business News magazine called the

extravaganza one of the "most unique" festivals in the country.

But pretend pirates aren't the only swashbucklers capturing international attention for the Tampa Bay area. Once assigned the dubious distinction as "America's Next Great City," Tampa has arrived as a premier player thanks in part to the Tampa Bay Buccaneers. Steered by coach Tony Dungy, the football team achieved worldwide respect and acclaim when the Buccaneers made the NFC playoffs. Hockey's Tampa Bay Lightning, soccer's Tampa Bay Mutiny and the arrival of the Tampa Bay Devil Rays baseball team also cinched the area's reputation as a major sports mecca. In 2001, Tampa again will be host to millions of football fans during Super Bowl XXXV.

Describing Tampa as "beautiful," "warm" and "friendly," tourists also applaud the "realness" and the "culture and heritage" the area offers, according to the Tampa/Hillsborough Convention and Visitors Association Inc. Our esteemed visitors are on target with such flattering impressions of the Tampa Bay area. But residents can relish another truth: The only experience better than visiting this land of sand, surf and sunsets is living here.

Tampa's skyline reflects the city's growth. The Tampa Bay region is a leader in business expansions, according to Southern Business & Development.

Photo by Steve Ribbe

Mayor Dick Greco, a native of Tampa, was the youngest mayor of a major U.S. city when he was elected in 1967 at 34. He served until 1973, resigning to join the Edward J. DeBartolo Corp. Two decades later, in 1995, he was re-elected as Tampa's top city official.

Photo by David Kadlubowski

Built in 1915, Tampa City Hall

keeps time with a clock

named Hortense.

Photo by Candace C. Mundy

Opened in 1926 and listed on the National Register of Historic Places, the Tampa Theatre is a restored movie palace presenting films, concerts and special events.

Photo by Steve Ribbe

Morning fog settles over downtown Tampa. On a clear day, Tampa's skyline can be viewed from a 20-mile radius.

Photo by Jock Fistick

Downtown scenes from top:

Newly renovated Tampa Union

Station, Harbour Island and

Sacred Heart Catholic Church.

Photos: (top and center) Steve

Ribbe; (bottom) Jim Reed

A pilot in Zephyrhills prepares

his hot air balloon for takeoff.

Photo by Pam Higgins

Jane Elizabeth Watts tries to

fly her handmade kite as she

runs down the sidewalk in

front of her Hyde Park home.

Photo by Jock Fistick

Tampa Bay Buccaneer Mike

Alstott heads to the end zone

past an upended Green Bay

Packer during the NFC

Divisional Playoff in January

1998 in Green Bay, Wis.

Photo by David Kadlubowski

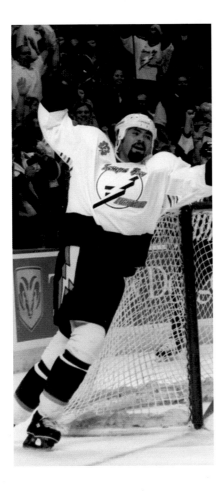

The Tampa Bay area is a major sports mecca for hockey, soccer, baseball and football. From left are the Tampa Bay Lightning, Tampa Bay Mutiny and Tampa Bay Devil Rays.

Photos: (left and center) Jim Reed, (right) Mark Guss

A cow in a meadow, a country

windmill and beach flowers

create serene scenes in the

Tampa Bay area.

Photos from left: Candace C.

Mundy, Bob Croslin, Bob Falcetti

A lone dog trots along the beach on Davis Islands during one of Tampa's sensational sunsets.

Photo by John W. Parker

The Florida Aquarium in Tampa is home to native wildlife, including turtles, birds, fish, river otters and other creatures.

Photo by Steve Ribbe

Tampa is becoming a player in

the cruise ship industry,

offering destinations including

Cozumel, Grand Cayman

Island and the Bahamas.

Photo by Steve Ribbe

Jazz great Nat Adderly cradles

his cornet in the record room

of his Lakeland home.

Photo by Greg Fight

Emily Kass, director of the Tampa Museum of Art, helps bring diverse exhibits, from classical displays to works by Bay area artists, to Tampa.

Photo by Andrew McKenzie

At Caffé Italia Ristorante in south Tampa, owner Andrea G. Fenu specializes in fresh, homemade pasta, left. Tracey Nolan is co-owner of Ovo Café, a trendy, late-night spot in Ybor City.

Photos by Andrew McKenzie

Clockwise, from top left: Wine sommelier Ken Collura is proud of the extensive selection of wine at Bern's Steak House in south Tampa. Vince McGilvra and Tom White are co-owners of Skipper's Smokehouse, a Tampa favorite. Rita Carlino of Carlino's on Bayshore shows off her famous chicken salad. Jack Whiteside is a co-owner of The Colonnade, a seafood restaurant and Tampa landmark on Bayshore Boulevard.

Photos by Andrew McKenzie

Strawberries are planted in

autumn and are ready for

picking in winter, just in

time for the annual

Florida Strawberry Festival

in Plant City.

Photo by Robert Burke

Strawberries and oranges are important agricultural products for the Tampa Bay area.

Photos by Robert Burke

The University of Tampa

Spartans challenge the

University of South Florida

Bulls during a soccer match.

Photo by Scott Martin

The University of South Florida Bulls made gridiron history on Sept. 6, 1997, as the first season of football added to the school's already large athletics department, which includes a number of coed sports.

Photo by Scott Martin

A fisherman casts his net at

Coon's Creek on MacDill

Air Force Base in Tampa.

Photo by Candace C. Mundy

A cyclist tours Flatwoods Park

in north Tampa.

Photo by Candace C. Mundy

Slot machines run 24 hours a

day at Seminole Indian Casino

in Tampa.

Photo by Robert Burke

Baseball spring training can be the best time for autograph seekers to catch their favorite players.

Photo by David Kadlubowski

It's a nice day for a wet wedding: Twelve couples took the plunge into matrimony in the Endless Surf Wave pool at Tampa's Adventure Island. Ralondo Herrera and Jacqueline Britt, foreground, seal their vows with a kiss.

Photo by David Kadlubowski

Water lovers prepare to fly on a flume at Tampa's Adventure Island, a water theme park near Busch Gardens.

Photo by Andrew McKenzie

Head Coach Tony Dungy leads

the Tampa Bay Buccaneers.

Photo by David Kadlubowski

Wade Boggs, left, Fred

McGriff and their Devil Rays

teammates brought Major

League Baseball to the

Tampa Bay area.

Photo by David Kadlubowski

Members of the Davis Island

Yacht Club's Dinghy Dames

negotiate a racecourse

during practice.

Photo by David Kadlubowski

A couple walks along the surf
at Fort DeSoto Park beach.
The beach has been named
one of the top 20 beaches in
the United States.

Photo by David Kadlubowski/Eagle 8

The Florida Aquarium's shark

exhibit showcases a variety of

the large fish, native to

Florida waters.

Photo by Jock Fistick

A National Geographic photographer films one of Florida's endangered manatees at Tampa's Lowry Park Zoo, one of three manatee rehabilitation hospitals in the state.

Photo by Gary Rings

Tampa's skyline lights up

the night.

Photo by Steve Ribbe

Floats, food, fairs and boats
are featured during Tampa's
annual extravaganzas
including Gasparilla, clockwise
from top left, the Florida State
Fair, the Knights of Sant' Yago
Night Parade and A Taste of
Florida.

Photos: (clockwise from top left)

Fred Bellet/Eagle 8, Bob Falcetti,

Jay Nolan, Steve Ribbe

Students at Harrison Center for the Visual and Performing Arts rehearse at the Harrison Center Theater on the campus of Lakeland High School.

Photo by Scott Iskowitz

Bealsville artist Ruby C. Williams' primitive folk art creations have achieved international status. She sells her paintings from her produce stand on State Road 60 near Plant City.

Photo by Robert Burke

The Rough Riders saddle up

in period costume,

reflecting the days of

Teddy Roosevelt and the

Spanish-American War.

Photo by Matt Larson

Civil War re-enactors gather at the University of Tampa's Plant Hall in preparation for the Saber and Rose Ball, left. Each year, lords and ladies converge with jugglers, jousters and knights in armor during the Renaissance Festival in Largo.

Photos from left: Jock Fistick, Fred Fox

Stretching 15 miles, the

Sunshine Skyway connects

St. Petersburg and Bradenton,

left. Soothing surf and fine

white sand attract visitors

to world-famous

Clearwater Beach.

Photos by Bob Croslin/Eagle 8

Powerboats blastoff from

The Pier during St. Petersburg's

Hurricane Offshore Classic.

Photo by Fred Fox/Eagle 8

Local businessman John Sykes, who never graduated from college himself, donated $10 million to the University of Tampa — the largest donation in its history.

Photo by Jim Reed

Gwendolyn W. Stephenson,

president of Hillsborough

Community College, oversees

more than 43,000 students

at the two-year school.

Photo by Matt Larson

Carriage rides are a popular

attraction in Old Hyde Park

Village, which has a "small

town" feel with quaint homes,

shopping and dining.

Photo by Matt Larson

One may wine and dine in SoHo (South Howard Avenue) with Charlie Inman Sr. of Charlie's Wine Cellar and SoHo Wine Bar, left, and Matt Hoffman, owner of Jim Strickland's Old Meeting House.

Photos from left: Candace C. Mundy, Andrew McKenzie

Tampa's Hyatt Regency

Westshore is an example of

the area's excellent

visitor accommodations.

Photo by Matt Larson

The Don CeSar Beach Resort and Spa on St. Pete Beach, left, had its heyday in the 1930s and continues to draw famous people from all over the world. The Renaissance Vinoy Resort, built in 1925, has been restored to its original beauty in downtown St. Petersburg.

Photos by Steve Ribbe/Eagle 8

Diving into cool water helps

beat the heat on a warm

summer day.

Photo by Karen Fletcher

Net fishing off Hernando County's Alfred A. McKethan Park is a relaxing way to spend an afternoon.

Photo by Fred Bellet

A tugboat passes by the
downtown Tampa skyline as it
makes its way down the
Hillsborough River toward the
Port of Tampa.

Photo by Jock Fistick

Tampa boasts the eighth

largest tonnage port in the

United States and the largest

deep-water port in Florida.

Photos from left: Jock Fistick,

Matt Larson

"The All New Captain Kangaroo" television show, starring John McDonough, is taped in the Tampa Bay area.

Photo provided by THCVA

"Titanic: The Exhibition" drew a record-breaking 830,019 visitors to the Florida International Museum in St. Petersburg. Other exhibits have included "Treasures of the Czars," "Alexander the Great," "Splendors of Ancient Egypt" and "Empires of Mystery: The Incas, The Andes and Lost Civilizations."

Photo by Mark Guss

Williams/Lunch On Limoges in Dade City is a favorite lunch spot for locals and visitors. Co-owners Skip Mize, left, and Phil Williams serve gourmet food and sell eclectic treasures as well as women's high-end fashions.

Photo by Matt Larson

The Dade City Courthouse,

left, and the 103-year-old

Mount Zion AME Church, led

by Pastor Nathan Mugala,

represent Dade City's history,

heritage and soul.

Photos from left: Matt Larson,

Pam Higgins

Officials on Egmont Key mark the shell of every turtle and tortoise to keep track of the local population.

Photo by Mark Guss

Egmont Key is a barrier island

at the mouth of Tampa Bay

and a sanctuary for turtles

and tortoises.

Photo by Selbypic

"Lightning," the 12-ton, 75-foot steel sculpture in front of Tampa's Ice Palace, is the tallest sculpture in the state of Florida.

Photo by Steve Ribbe

The charm and character of a community are illustrated through acclaimed artist Josette Urso's five-panel "The Plant City Story (Memory) Quilt," which is on permanent display at the County Courthouse Annex in Plant City.

Photo by Robert Burke

Tampa Stadium, right, played

host to two Super Bowls:

XVIII and XXV. The new

Raymond James Stadium will

welcome football fans for

Super Bowl XXXV in 2001.

Photo by Todd Chappel

The Devil Rays infected the
Tampa Bay area with baseball
fever during the team's
inaugural game, March 31,
1998, at Tropicana Field
in St. Petersburg.

Photo by Jay Conner

Cypress domes in the

Keystone area show off

Florida's natural beauty.

Photo by Jim Reed

West Central Florida is called

"the lightning capital of

the nation."

Photo by Fred Bellet

Judith Lisi, executive director of the Tampa Bay Performing Arts Center, is responsible for the success of the center, bringing big Broadway shows such as "Phantom of the Opera," "Sunset Boulevard," "Chicago," "Rent" and "Miss Saigon."

Photo by Matt Larson

Cameron Mackintosh's "Les Misérables" has graced the stage at the Tampa Bay Performing Arts Center to sold-out audiences.

Photo provided by Tampa Bay Performing Arts Center

A crowd follows golfer

John Daly during the

J.C. Penney Classic at

Innisbrook Resort in

Palm Harbor.

Photo by Fred Fox

Spanning six miles, Tampa's Bayshore Boulevard is one of the world's longest continuous sidewalks and is popular with joggers, cyclists, skaters and dog walkers.

Photo by Phil Sheffield

Comical feats and twists

reached new heights when

Ringling Bros. and Barnum &

Bailey Circus clowns

visited Busch Gardens

for a roller coaster ride.

Photo provided by Busch Gardens

For more than 40 years, Busch Gardens has amused visitors with exotic entertainment, awesome animals and thrilling rides. Bottom: Deija Parker keeps the beat with her dad, Donnie Parker, during Take Our Daughters To Work Day at the theme park.

Photos from top: Provided by Busch Gardens, Candace C. Mundy, Karen Fletcher

Art and archives are alive
and well-preserved in
St. Petersburg. Michael
Milkovich, left, is the director
of The Museum of Fine Arts.
And visitors admire works of
surrealist Salvador Dalí
at the museum named
for him.

Photos by Steve Ribbe

The University of South Florida's Contemporary Art Museum brings in works by artists emerging on the national and international fronts, left. The Henry B. Plant Museum, at the University of Tampa, showcases original antiques from the 1891-era Tampa Bay Hotel.

Photos from left: Andrew McKenzie, George Cott/Chroma Inc.

Ybor City celebrities, from left:

Mama and Papa Guava reign

supreme during Guavaween;

Joe Roman sings with your

supper at the Columbia

Restaurant; and Marina Lopez

performs at Fiesta Day.

Photos from left: Bob Croslin,

Jim Reed, Jay Nolan

Rosann Garcia displays cigars at the Ybor City State Museum, left. Every weekend, the Ybor City Ghost Walk guides spirit seekers through Ybor City's past.

Photos from left: Steve Ribbe, Michael Murphy

A St. Petersburg landmark,

The Coliseum ballroom has

offered swing for the soul

since 1924.

Photo by Kevin Howe

Florida's largest independent bookstore, Haslam's, was established in 1933. Pictured are three generations of the Haslam family, from left: Raymond V. Hinst Jr., Suzanne Haslam Hinst, Elizabeth Haslam and Raymond V. Hinst III.

Photo by Steve Ribbe

Tampa International Airport repeatedly has won acclaim from the Airline Passengers Association as one of the top airports in the United States.

Photo by Matt Larson

A great destination for pilots and passengers, the Tampa Bay area stages annual fly-ins, introducing a variety of military and specialty aircraft to thousands of flight fans.

Photos from left: David Kadlubowski, Cliff McBride

Canoeists glide past a

sunbathing alligator on the

Hillsborough River.

Photo by Karen Fletcher

The sun sets off the rustic

fishing village of Cedar Key.

Photo by Fred Fox

The Tampa Convention Center
is a world-class meeting
space, which also brings
events such as the Florida
International New Car Show
and motivational speakers.

Photo by Steve Ribbe

MOSI (the Museum of Science & Industry) is the largest science center in the Southeastern United States and home to an IMAX Dome Theater.

Photo by George Cott/Chroma Inc.

Near downtown Tampa,

Howard W. Blake High School

is a magnet school for the

visual, performing and

communication arts.

Photo by David Kadlubowski/Eagle 8

Built in 1927, Hillsborough

High School is the second

oldest high school in

Hillsborough County.

Photo by Steve Ribbe

Wildlife conservationist,

primatologist and researcher

Jane Goodall shares a quiet

moment with a gorilla in the

Myombe Reserve at Busch

Gardens in Tampa.

Photo by Candace C. Mundy

Tampa's Lowry Park Zoo

brings in animals from all over

the world, including white

lions, red pandas and

Komodo dragons.

Photo by Jay Nolan

A full moon illuminates the

University of Tampa's

minarets in this double-

exposure photograph.

Photo by Jim Reed

An astronomer takes

advantage of the clear country

sky to stargaze in Brooksville.

Photo by Andy Jones

At sunrise, a flock of birds takes off across a cloud-filled sky at Edward Medard Park at Turkey Creek in eastern Hillsborough County.

Photo by Dave Geiger

The sun descends on another

beautiful day over Tarpon Key,

near the Sunshine Skyway.

Photo by Mark Guss

Credits

Publisher – Reid Ashe

Marketing Communications Director – Michael Kilgore

Project Coordinator and Photo Editor – Matt Larson

Creative Manager – Paul Wright

Designer – Lana Burroughs

Editor – Donna Strickland

Writer – Kathy Feeney

Copy Editors – Avril de Aristizábal, Nitish S. Rele, Vickie Romanowski,

Gail Cadow Schomers and Marti Wiggins

University of Tampa Press Director – Richard Mathews

Special thanks to Richard Catalano, Kevin Foley, Larry Hutchinson, Bill Stivali, Greg Stewart, Leland Hawes and Eagle 8.

"TAMPA AND WEST CENTRAL FLORIDA: POSTCARD PARADISE" IS PUBLISHED BY THE TAMPA TRIBUNE WITH THE UNIVERSITY OF TAMPA PRESS.

FIRST EDITION
ISBN 1-879852-60-8
LIBRARY OF CONGRESS NUMBER 98-87189

PRINTED IN CHINA